M000075969

BUILD YOUR CONSULTING PRACTICE

HOW INDEPENDENT CONSULTANTS
DELIVER VALUE TO CLIENTS AND
GROW THEIR BUSINESS

HENRY DEVRIES & MARK LEBLANC

INDIE BOOKS
INTERNATIONAL

Copyright © 2017 by Henry DeVries and Mark LeBlanc
All rights reserved.
Printed in the United States of America.

No part of this publication may be reproduced or distributed in any form
or by any means without the prior permission of the publisher. Requests
for permission should be directed to permissions@indiebooksintl.com or
mailed to Permissions, Indie Books International, 2424 Vista Way, Suite 316,
Oceanside, CA 92054.

Neither the publisher nor the author is engaged in rendering legal or other
professional services through this book. If expert assistance is required, the
services of appropriate professionals should be sought. The publisher and
the author shall have neither liability nor responsibility to any person or
entity with respect to any loss or damage caused directly or indirectly by the
information in this publication.

ISBN-10: 1-941870-85-6
ISBN-13: 978-1-941870-85-3
Library of Congress Control Number: 2017910344

Designed by Joni McPherson, mcphersongraphics.com

INDIE BOOKS INTERNATIONAL, LLC
2424 VISTA WAY, SUITE 316
OCEANSIDE, CA 92054
www.indiebooksintl.com

*To our parents, Jack and Janice DeVries and
Ralph and Lois LeBlanc, and to our wives,
Vikki DeVries and Ann LeBlanc*

CONTENTS

PREFACE

THE BIGGEST MYSTERY

Riding the revenue roller coaster has never been a fun ride.

The biggest mystery for independent consultants is how to attract high-paying clients on a regular and consistent basis. There are plenty of clues that point to a solution: you have to get your head screwed on right when it comes to money, focus, and marketing.

Ironically, many independent consultants feel business development is too time consuming, expensive, or undignified. Even if they try a business development program, most professionals, consultants, and small business owners are frustrated by a lack of results. They even worry whether business development would ever work for them.

No wonder they are doubtful and worried. According to a former professor and author from the Harvard Business School, David Maister, the typical sales and marketing hype that works for retailers and manufacturers is not only a waste of time and money for professionals and consultants, it actually makes them less attractive to prospective clients.

But research shows there is a better way. There are proven processes for business development with integrity that generate up to a 400 percent to 2000 percent return on your investment. We call these the *Educating Expert Model* (developed by Henry DeVries) and the *Nine Best Practices* (developed by Mark LeBlanc), and the most successful professional service and consulting firms use these processes to attract more high-paying clients than they can handle.

What should you do to increase revenues? First, understand that generating prospects is an investment and should be measured like any other investment. Next, quit wasting money on ineffective means like brochures, advertising, and sponsorships. The best business development investment you can make is to create informative websites, host persuasive seminars, book speaking engagements, and get published as a blog columnist and eventually as the author of a book.

And, oh, most importantly, spend nine minutes a day making a phone call, sending an e-mail, and dropping a card in the mail. We call these high-value activities.

Think of high-value activities like One-A-Day vitamins for your business: one phone call, one e-mail, and one snail mail a day: One a day, one a day, one a day.

Henry DeVries and Mark LeBlanc

April, 2017

PART I

CRACKING THE CODE WITH NINE BEST PRACTICES

". . . and, therefore, I share my Nobel Prize with my consultant."

Based on our research, the code has been cracked. There is a group of successful independent consultants who no longer struggles with the ups and downs of the revenue roller coaster. To help you crack the code, this book is a how-to guide that takes the mystery out of business development with pragmatic advice in three areas: money, focus, and marketing. Follow the nine best practices in this trio of matters, and you will succeed. Here is a quick overview:

MONEY

1. **Track Your Numbers Properly.** There are many tips in this book; this is the only demandment.

2. **Know Your Numbers.** What gets measured gets managed. If you are unwilling to consider going on QuickBooks and reshaping your profit-and-loss statement, you should probably quit reading now.

FOCUS

1. **Create a Profile of Your Ideal Week.** Good news, everybody. You don't control much in life, but you do get to control your time. Isn't that why you became an independent professional, solo consultant, or small business owner in the first place?

2. **Maintain Your Daily Focus.** Mighty castles are built one brick at a time. All we ask is nine minutes a day to make a call, send an e-mail, and mail a card. One a day, one a day, one a day.

3. **Develop Your Will-Do List.** Scrap those traditional "to-do" lists. Instead, what three accomplishments will you complete in thirty days, ninety days, in one year, in five years, and in ten years? These are the stars you guide your ship by.

MARKETING

1. **Execute a Mix of New Contact Strategies.** There are no bad marketing strategies. Everyone is unique, and everyone needs a mix that works for him or her. "One size fits all" is one of the world's three great lies (the other two are "This won't hurt as much as you think," and "I'm from the government, and I am here to help.")

2. **Leverage Your Database.** Next to cash, this is the biggest asset your business has. The time has come to whip your lazy database into shape.

3. **Navigate Your Internet Game Plan.** It is a brave new digital world. Beware: does your web presence make you look old and outdated?

4. Listen Carefully, Respond Appropriately. At last, you are having a meaningful conversation with a prospect. Most independent professionals and solo consultants can increase their closing rates by 50 to 100 percent based on how they ask and answer questions.

The more prospects you inform how to solve their problems in general, the more will hire you for the specifics. In the words of the late motivational speaker Zig Ziglar: "You can get whatever you want in life if you just help enough people get what they want."

To get what you want is going to take money. On to Part II to consider that very subject.

PART II

MONEY

Money is the best place to start. That is because money is the greatest catalyst for making better decisions. If the money part of your business does not add up, nothing else is going to add up either.

Getting the money side right is not about greed; far from it. Most consultants are driven by a desire to serve and bring insight to those with problems. However, unless you get the money part of your business right, you will not be able to stay in business.

The concept is called *sacred selfishness*. For you to be able to serve others, you must first take care of yourself. This is akin to when you are about to take off as a passenger on an airline, and the flight attendant explains that in the unlikely event of a loss of cabin pressure, oxygen masks will drop down. If you are traveling with small children or the elderly, your number one job is to put the oxygen mask on yourself first, and then proceed to help others. Reversing the order can be fatal for all.

Another metaphor is the soup kettle. If you want to share soup with others, you'd better make sure you fill your pot with good ingredients. If you fail to nourish yourself with soup, there will be no chef to nourish others and no soup to share.

So how do consultants and professionals get the money side wrong? First, they think about money on an annual basis. Yearly goals, objectives, and benchmarks do not serve you well. Instead, transform your thinking to consider money on a monthly basis.

Money comes in on a monthly basis and money goes out on a monthly basis. Your mortgage, rent, utility bills, loan payments and the like are paid monthly. Think about your business in the same manner.

What you need is a path and a plan to have a model month. The secret to success is to replicate the ideal month over and over. Executing this path and plan increases the likelihood—note the word likelihood— of having a model month. One key to success is adjusting your thinking to thirty-day increments.

1

TRACK YOUR NUMBERS PROPERLY

"I didn't go to Harvard, I didn't go to Stanford, and you won't find a bunch of letters after my name," says independent consultant Craig Lowder.

"I once went as far as having MBA on my business card, but you won't find it there anymore. Mine was a blue-collar family just outside the rust belt, where I learned that it's not only what you know, but how you apply it. I learned a couple of other important lessons back then that still serve me today."

This is a man who has built his practice around the concept of tracking his numbers.

Lowder, who hails from Chicago, is a sales-effectiveness expert with a thirty-year track record of helping owners of small and midsize companies achieve their sales goals. He has worked with more than fifty companies and increased first-year annual sales by 22 to 142 percent.

A turning point in building his consulting practice was collecting data and sharing his research in speeches and then in a book.

"Selling is a science that must be artfully executed," is the message Lowder is spreading to companies with stalled growth.

"Like any other science, there are scientific sales principles to follow," says Lowder in his 2016 book, *Smooth Selling Forever: Charting Your Company's Course for Predictable and Sustainable Sales Growth.*[1]

"Over the past three decades I have studied dozens and dozens of small to midsize companies where the selling was not smooth," says Lowder. "Patterns began to emerge as to why sales were not growing as expected."

One pattern for stalled companies and consultants is a failure to properly track numbers.

No book that claims to have unraveled a mystery would be complete without some lab-tested formulas.

---

[1] Lowder, Craig. *Smooth Selling Forever: Charting Your Company's Course for Predictable and Sustainable Sales Growth.* Oceanside, CA: Indie Books International, 2016.

Actually, two formulas are essential to getting the money side right: the SRO formula and the 50/35/15 formula.

Our laboratory has been the make-it-or-break-it world of independent consulting in the United States and Canada. These formulas have been field-tested with more than one thousand independent professionals and solo consultants over the past two decades.

The first step for your path and plan to track your numbers properly is to determine your SRO numbers: *S* stands for survival, *R* stands for realistic, and *O* stands for optimistic.

In the words of the Roman statesman Seneca, "If one does not know what harbor one is making for, no wind is the right wind." Or as baseball Hall-of-Famer Yogi Berra put it, "If you don't know where you are going, you better be careful, because you might not get there."

Tracking your numbers properly starts with a business development goal number for how much revenue you want to book. Here is how to determine that number.

The process begins with determining your survival number. How much money do you need to generate on a monthly basis to survive? This means paying yourself, paying your taxes, generating leads, and paying for office supplies.

The process then continues with looking at a larger number—what we call the realistic number. As a benchmark, think about what you generated in the last twelve months and then divide that by twelve for your monthly average. Some months might have been great, and some might have been terrible. But what was the average monthly number last year and the year before that? This is probably your realistic number.

Now think bigger. How much would you have to generate on average on a monthly basis to get excited about? This is an amount of billings you could manage to service and still have balance in your life. In other words, there would still be time to take care of your health, your relationships, and the fun in your life. Personally, we prefer to have our fun meters set on max.

OPTIMISTIC NUMBER DEFINITION

> *Your optimistic number is the number that represents the dollar volume of work you want to book in a month, at your current fee levels, with your fun meter on max, having the kind of balance you want between your home and work life.*

Here is an example of how to calculate an optimistic number. One consultant we worked with said she had averaged $84,000 per year for the past two years. She said her goal was to double that and make $168,000 for the year. This means her realistic number was $7,000 a month. Her optimistic number was $14,000 a month.

"But," she said, "I have organized my business to only work ten months out of the year.

What should my optimistic number be?"

Brava. In this case, she would simply divide by ten. So, her monthly realistic number should be $8,400, and her optimistic number is $16,800.

There is no right or wrong answer for your optimistic number. This is up to you. The only wrong answer is not to have one.

THE 50/35/15 FORMULA

While the SRO formula is a revenue side of the equation approach, the 50/35/15 formula is focused on the expense side of the business. This is a baseline formula that has worked for small businesses in the $100,000-to-$2 million annual-revenue range.

The formula advises independent professionals, solo consultants, and small business owners how to allocate net revenues after the cost of sales is subtracted from the gross revenues. The 50 translates to 50 percent for ODI (owner's discretionary income); 35 means 35 percent for business development; and 15 represents 15 percent for office administration expenses. This is your road map to expense management.

Now, every business is unique. The perfect formula for you might end up being 60/30/10 or 55/25/20. In the beginning, however, until you get twelve months of benchmarks under your belt, the recommended course is to aim for an allocation of 50/35/15.

Let's begin the discussion with the 50 percent for ODI. Business owners take compensation in many forms: a salary, a draw, health insurance, life insurance, disability insurance, automobile loan payment or lease, your SEP IRA or another retirement amount. (Plus, don't forget taxes.)

The 35 percent for business development covers such costs as advertising, direct mail, publicity, attending networking events, putting on seminars, publishing a book, maintaining a website, professional development, and other promotional activities that are new client contact strategies and tools. You must invest time and resources if you want to grow your business.

The 15 percent is for office administration. To grow in the sweet spot, you are probably going to need some help. This would cover an actual or virtual assistant, office space, computers, software, tax and legal help, stationery, and the like. An assistant can free you up to focus on the necessary tasks of sales and marketing for your business, not to mention servicing clients.

Depending on your business model, you also cannot ignore the cost of sales. If your business model includes a direct cost to manufacture a product or a labor cost that you include to create the service you offer, that is called cost of sales (sometimes called COGS, or cost of goods sold), which is deducted from revenues before the formula is applied.

For example, a business might look something like this. The monthly optimistic number for a graphic designer is $12,000, and the monthly cost of sales is $2,000 (subcontracting to a graphic artist). After the $2,000 is subtracted from the $12,000, the formula is applied to the remaining $10,000. The owner keeps 50 percent, or $5,000, as a monthly salary. Another 35 percent, or $3,500, is invested in business development. The remaining 15 percent, or $1,500, is spent on office admin, including rent for a studio and a virtual assistant and a part-time bookkeeper.

Gross revenue	$12,000
Cost of sales	2,000
Net revenue	$10,000
ODI	5,000
Business development	3,500
Office admin	1,500
Net profit	**0**

SIDE BY SIDE BY SIDE

A third step in tracking your numbers properly is to record three key numbers in three columns on a spreadsheet: your booking number, your bank deposits, and your ODI. Record these side by side by side, day by day by day.

Bookings by Profit Center	Bank Deposits	ODI Taken Out
$2,500 (Logo design)	$1,000	$500

The booking number is a sales number that is recorded when a prospect agrees to become a client, and there is a meeting of the minds on a dollar amount. Record this on the day the sale is booked, not when payment is received. The amount may be for a year-long contract that is paid out on a monthly basis. Record the entire contract amount in the left column.

The sum of these booking numbers provides the total booking number for the month, which is compared to the optimistic number. The goal is to meet or exceed the optimistic number on a monthly basis. But understand that all business booked will probably not turn into revenue. A natural part of business is that there is some leakage.

The booking column can be more robust. The booking column can be split into subcolumns that represent booking profit centers. Professionals and consultants typically have multiple revenue streams, including consulting fees, coaching fees, speaking fees, royalties, and product sales, just to name a few. Splitting the column into subcolumns, allows an owner to track various profit centers.

Now the spreadsheet should look more like this:

Day of the Month	Profit Center 1	Profit Center 2	Profit Center 3	Profit Center 4	Bank Deposits	ODI Taken Out
1						
2						
3						
4						
5						
(and so on…)						
31						

The sixth column is for bank deposits. This is recorded when you receive the money and have access to it. The sum of all these deposits provides the gross revenue number for the month. There is a natural lag between bookings and revenues.

The third column is for ODI. This is where you record what you are taking out of the business. The spreadsheet can be simply programmed to provide the percentage of ODI that is being taken from revenues. Remember the 50/35/15 formula? This is a quick check to see if you're taking too much or too little to create a sustainable business.

The good news: you do not have to build your own spreadsheet. A great one has already been created, and it is our gift to you. If you would like a free copy of the Numbers Tracking Tool invented by Mark LeBlanc, please e-mail Henry at henry@indiebooksintl.com.

© Randy Glasbergen
www.glasbergen.com

*"The time management consultant just called to say he is
running a little late."*

2

KNOW YOUR NUMBERS

Margaret Reynolds began her career at Hallmark Cards, Inc., where she held executive roles of general manager and lead strategic officer, and was known for her natural inquisitiveness and innovative inclinations, never resting with the status quo.

She opened her independent consulting practice in Kansas City in 2001, and by 2008 had added a second office in Nashville.

What was the key to building the business? The answer is knowing the numbers.

Tracking leading indicators can provide an early warning system that is invaluable to any business, giving it more time to react and increasing the probability of achieving breakthrough growth.

"Leading indicators are measures of progress on key

variables that determine if the strategy is working," says Reynolds, author of the 2015 book *Reignite: How Everyday Companies Spark Next-Stage Growth.*[2] "The specific measures reflect the strategic choice made by the organization."

Sometimes as organizations track leading indicators and anticipate being off at year end, they will perform short-term heroics to supplement strategic results, such as holding a fire sale. Independent consultants are frequently tempted to do the same thing.

"While this may help in the short run, leading indicators suggest that implementation is not achieving the desired results and either the implementation effort is falling short or the strategy needs to be revisited," says Reynolds.

In order to make business a game worth playing, it pays to know the score. Knowing your numbers is one of the secrets to increasing your profitability and making smarter decisions on matters like pricing.

Some independent professionals, solo consultants,

---

[2] Reynolds, Margaret. *Reignite: How Everyday Companies Spark Next-stage Growth.* Oceanside, CA: Indie Book International, 2015.

and small business owners look at their profit and loss numbers once a year, when it is time to pull together revenues and expenses for taxes. Others are proud because they look at their numbers on a quarterly basis.

Sorry—not good enough.

Starting immediately, we recommend getting your finances on QuickBooks and looking at your P&L (profit and loss) statement on a monthly basis. By the fifteenth day of the following month, an owner should be able to see a P&L for the previous month, a P&L for the previous rolling twelve-month period that ends in that month, and a P&L for the prior year's rolling twelve-month period.

For example, let us say this is November 15, 2019. The owner would want to see a P&L for October 2019, another P&L for November 2018 through October 2019, and a final P&L for November 2017 through October 2018. In other words, last month, last year, and the previous year.

RESHAPE THAT PROFIT AND LOSS STATEMENT

Are you playing at business or playing to win? The winners do what it takes to get their finances on QuickBooks and reshape their P&L statements to match the 50/35/15 formula categories described in chapter one.

Typically, the QuickBooks program organizes expense categories in alphabetical order. Reshaping your P&L statement is a one-time process that will take little time. Follow these steps (or have your bookkeeper follow these steps) to reshape your QuickBooks:

Organize your Income section by profit center.

1. Group your Cost of Sales expenses together.

2. Group your ordinary Expenses into three categories: ODI, business development, and office administration.

3. Include all the ways you take money out for yourself in the ODI expense category.

4. Include all the expenses that you feel will ultimately help you grow or build your business in the Business Development category.

5. Include all the overhead and office expenses necessary for the day-to-day running of your business in the Office Administration category.

Please note this is a management accounting action and not a tax reporting action. The way the IRS or Revenue Canada wants these numbers reported is slightly different. But this is a simple once-a-year adjustment. The important task is to know your numbers on a monthly basis so you can make informed decisions about your business.

QuickBooks software has options for you to create a template for your reports. Reshaping your P&L statement helps an owner take advantage of the critical information needed at a moment's notice to make smarter decisions.

HOW TO DOUBLE REVENUES

If you are an independent consultant, then you need to focus on the revenue formula. We don't know who your ninth grade algebra teacher was and what your relationship was with him or her, but please stay with us. This is as easy as A times B plus C.

- A stands for new clients.

- *B* is how much you charge per new client.

- *C* is the amount of money you get from past clients.

- So, Revenue = (A × B) + C

Actually, there are two components to new clients: the number of qualified prospects you talk to multiplied by your conversion rate (CR). There are four types of prospects: suspects, tire kickers, referrals, and qualified prospects. Here are our definitions.

A *suspect* is one of the seven billion people on the earth you suspect might be interested in what you do, but all you have is a name and contact information.

A *tire kicker* is someone who has taken a step toward you and is interested in what you have to say. He or she may have attended a seminar, come to a speech, visited a trade show booth, signed up for your e-mail newsletter, asked for a copy of your white paper, or engaged in some other information-gathering activity.

A *referral* is someone whom one of your advocates suggested call you. This person has heard positive things about you and might call you one day.

Now, *qualified prospects* (QP) are tire kickers or referrals who call you and want to meet with you to hear how you might solve their problems (and how much you charge).

To recap, here are the formula components.

A = (#QP × CR%) = new clients

B = $ you get per new client

C = $ you get from current and past clients

To illustrate, let's say you talk to ten qualified prospects per month. You convert 20 percent (one out of five) into new clients. You charge each new client $1,000. Added to that, you get $3,000 a month from existing and past clients. (Oh no, a word problem. Don't panic or have traumatic school flashbacks. Please, stick with us.) You make $5,000 per month.

(10 × .20) ($1000) + $3000

(2) ($1000) + $3000

$2000 + $3000 = $5,000

But what if you could talk to fifteen qualified prospects per month instead of ten? What if you

could get $1,150 per client instead of $1,000? What if
you could convert two out of five (40 percent) instead
of one out of five? What if you could get $3,300 a
month (a 10 percent increase) from past and existing
clients instead of $3,000? All of these increases are
actually modest and very doable. See what happens
to revenue (yes, it more than doubles).

$(15 \times .4)\ (\$1,150) + \$3,300$

$(6)\ (\$1,150) + \$3,300$

$\$6,900 + \$3,300 = \$10,200$

Voila: You have doubled your revenues.

To recap, here is how to leverage the four factors:

- **Number of evaluators you talk to each month**.
Showcase your expertise by hosting seminars,
webinars, and teleseminars focused on client
pains that you address. Present research on
how they compare to their peers. Your book is a
credibility tool.

- **Percentage of evaluators you convert into
clients**. Use a lead conversion system where you
ask the right questions (can increase conversion

rates by 50 percent to 100 percent). Listen carefully and respond appropriately.

- **How much you charge each new client.** Experiment with three-tiered platinum/gold/ silver pricing strategies. Experts can charge more, and being an author helps make you an expert.

- **How much money you get from past and existing clients.** Ask about problems and offer options how to solve. Your best prospects are past clients.

PART III
FOCUS

"You've probably heard of me. I'm an author, consultant and lecturer in the fields of authoring, consulting and lecturing."

If you are an independent professional, solo consultant, or small business owner, here is the good and bad news: you are the boss of you.

When you brush your teeth in the morning and before you go to bed at night, the boss of your time is looking back at you in the bathroom mirror. Although the saying has become a cliché, there is still truth to the old adage, "failing to plan is planning to fail." What you do during a week should not be left to a to-do list and the tyranny of the urgent. You need to "plan the work and work the plan."

It was Gretchen Rubin, author of *The Happiness Project*, who observed: "The days are long and the years are short."

In business development terms, this means if you do not buy out the time to do what needs to be done to grow your business, another year will zip by before you know it. After each of those long days, you should ask yourself, "Did I trade this day for survival or my dreams?"

3

CREATE A PROFILE OF YOUR IDEAL WEEK

Paul Ratoff is a Certified Management Consultant who has been a successful independent business consultant in Southern California for the past thirty-five years, assisting a wide range of middle-market companies plan and manage their growth and success.

Everything he does, especially how he spends his time, has a purpose.

"Purposeful behavior means taking actions that are consistent with a purpose that is meaningful and important to all the organization's stakeholders," says Paul Ratoff, author of the 2016 book, *Thriving in a Stakeholder World: Purpose as the New Competitive Advantage.*[3]

---

3 Ratoff, Paul. *Thriving in a Stakeholder World: Purpose as the New Competitive Advantage.* Oceanside, CA: Indie Books International, 2016.

His book demonstrates to business leaders that purpose can be the driving force behind a better management style and also provide a competitive advantage in their markets.

Call us contrarians. Just because technology allows you to be connected 24/7/365 (twenty-four hours a day, seven days a week, three hundred sixty-five days a year) does not mean that you should be. We are staunch advocates for creating boundaries between work and home.

Return for a moment to the definition of the optimistic number from the first chapter. This is the number that represents the amount of business you want to book in a month at your current fee levels with your fun meter on max and maintaining *the kind of balance you want between your home and work life.*

President George W. Bush once said in a speech, "an entrepreneur is someone who would rather work eighty hours a week for themselves rather than work forty hours a week for someone else." Because of that independent streak, many will resist the practice of setting up an ideal week. But that is a miscalculation in thinking.

Creating an ideal week gives you more freedom, not more restrictions. There is a truism that work will expand to fill available space. So, if you do not set boundaries, ones that *you* impose, you will find activities you *want* to do crowded out by activities you feel you *must* do.

Here is how the ideal week (and month) works. If you want a business model that you are excited about, creating an ideal week is a great place to start.

Start with a five-day, Monday-to-Friday week (although you can expand this out to a seven-day week if you wish). When would you like to do the following?

- Start your work day

- End your work day

- Meet with clients

- Prep for client meetings

- Service clients

- Meet with prospective clients (perhaps for coffee)

- Attend networking meetings to prospect

- Engage in marketing

- Make three high-value phone calls during the day

- Exercise

- Engage in recreation

- Learn or take part in education

- Pray, meditate, or otherwise refill your spiritual tank

The term is "ideal" week and month because invariably, some days and weeks will not be ideal. The concept, however, is to have an ideal to strive for and attempt to shape where possible how you allocate your time.

As a starting point, consider a weekly chart that looks something like this. This is designed with eight two-hour blocks and an eight-hour block for sleeping.

	Sun	Mon	Tue	Wed	Thur	Fri	Sat
6:00 to 8:00 a.m.							
8:00 to 10:00 a.m.							
10:000 to 12:00 p.m.							
12:00 to 2:00 p.m.							
2:00 to 4:00 p.m.							
4:00 to 6:00 p.m.							
6:00 to 8:00 p.m.							
8:00 to 10:00 p.m.							
10:00 to 6:00 a.m.							

You might be an early riser. Maybe your day starts at 5:00 a.m. with exercise and meditation. Perhaps you like to start the work day at 7:00 a.m. and end at 5:00 p.m. Perhaps you are not a morning person, and you would rather get up later. You can start the day later and end it later; it is your choice. You may have an afternoon or day of the week that is sacred, and nothing gets scheduled during that time. You have the power.

For Kylie Strem, an independent contractor who works for Mark from her home, the ideal week made a huge difference. Kylie is the mother of three young children. When the children returned home from elementary school each day, she would get them a snack and return to work for another hour or so. Her work-and-home balance greatly improved when she decided that her work day would end at 3:30 p.m., when her children's school bus arrived. She could then focus on the children and interact with them about their day.

MAINTAIN YOUR DAILY FOCUS

The problem with life is it is so daily. Get up, get busy, get tired, and get to bed. Before you know it, days and weeks and months pass.

But what did you do on a consistent and persistent basis to make payroll? The fourth best practice is to have your day begin with a morning ritual.

THE A.M. QUESTION

Begin the day by opening the numbers tracking tool, looking at your optimistic number for the month, and then asking yourself the a.m. question: *"What am I doing today to book my optimistic number?"* Write down three high-value activities for the day.

That is the focus of the day. "What am I doing today to

book my optimistic number?" The optimistic number is your sales goal for the month, and it is not going to book itself. The pressures of doing work for clients can crowd it out of your daily duties. Don't let it. You are in charge, so take a moment in the still of the morning at home to create a short will-do list.

Do not screw this up by being creative and coming up with your own version of the question. This is not the time for creativity. Don't deviate from the script. We repeat it for emphasis: *"What am I doing today to book my optimistic number?"*

Mark was working with a consultant for ten years before he finally realized she was asking the wrong a.m. question. She was asking, "What are my high-value activities for the day?" It is amazing how easy it is to get off-track. That is a different question that produces a different result. What is wrong with that question? She failed to connect her plan for the day to her optimistic number.

The important aspect of this daily ritual is to connect your a.m. question to your optimistic number. Of course, the next step is to write down three high-value activities for the day that will help you book that optimistic number. But the first focus should be on the number.

How do you make it rain high-paying clients? With the storm-starter strategy, tied to your optimistic number. The storm-starter strategy is about daily actions, done on a consistent basis, to attract high-paying clients.

A high-value activity is a storm-starter call, e-mail, or card. Do all three—call, e-mail, and snail mail—on a daily basis, and the storm starts brewing. Before long, the forecast will be 90 percent chance of raining new clients.

As part of the daily ritual, write down your three high-value activities (your HVAs) for the day and then do them. Executing the three high-value activities will only take you nine minutes a day, but those are the most important nine minutes of the day.

Like a One-A-Day vitamin, the storm-starter strategy requires that you do each variety of activity every day. A call a day. An e-mail a day. A mailing a day. One a day, one a day, one a day.

Here is what a high-value activity is *not*: By this daily focus definition, writing your blog is not a high-value activity. Writing your e-mail newsletter is not a high-value activity. Writing your upcoming speech is not a high-value activity. These are all extremely important, and they need to be prioritized somewhere in your day. But they are not the most important activities that will lead you to booking your optimistic number on a monthly basis.

Your day should end with another daily ritual: The P.M. Question.

THE P.M. QUESTION

End the day by opening up the tracking tool, looking at your optimistic number for the month, and then asking yourself the p.m. question: *"What did I do today to book my optimistic number?"* Did you accomplish the three high-value activities you committed to in the morning? Be accountable to yourself.

DEVELOP YOUR WILL-DO LIST

For years, writing a book was a building-your-practice dream for Penny Reed. It became a reality when she put it on her will-do list.

"If a dentist has been in practice for any length of time, they've likely read dozens, if not hundreds, of articles on how to grow your practice, and many offer conflicting advice," says Penny, an independent dental consultant and author of the 2015 book, *Growing Your Dental Practice: Market Yourself Effectively and Accelerate Your Results.*[4]

"The purpose of my book is to direct dentists' focus to the five most important areas that drive growth in their business and how their role as a business owner, leader, and coach influence these key areas. This is especially important as dental reimbursement

---

[4] Reed, Penny. *Growing Your Dental Business: Market Yourself Effectively and Accelerate Your Results.* California: Indie Books International, 2015.

continues to be flat causing increased pressure to find proactive ways to grow their practice."

Based in Memphis, Tennessee, Reed has worked with dentists and spoken to dental groups for over twenty-five years. Her articles have been published in numerous trade publications including *Dental Economics, Dentistry Today,* and *Inside Dentistry.* She was selected by *Dentistry Today* as one of their prestigious Leaders in Dental Consulting from 2007 to 2016.

The will-do list is the easiest of the nine best practices. No doubt you have a master to-do list. All this step asks is that you segment the list.

Create a master to-do list for growing your business and your personal life, then segment it into the seven categories listed below. This can be done in a word-processing document or a spreadsheet.

1. Section number one is your **thirty-day segment**.

2. Section number two is your **ninety-day segment**.

3. Section number three your **twelve-month segment**.

4. Section number four is your **five-year segment.**

5. Section number five is your **ten-year segment.**

6. Section number six is your **parking lot.**

7. Section number seven is your **accomplishments.**

	Growing Your Business	**Personal**
Thirty-day		
Ninety-day		
Twelve-month		
Five-year		
Ten-year		
Parking lot		
Accomplishments		

Do the following planning exercise every thirty days:

1. Write three action items you are willing to commit to in your business life and personal life in the next thirty days in the two **thirty-day boxes.**

2. Write three action items you are willing to commit to in your business life and personal life in the

next ninety days in the two **ninety-day boxes.**

3. Write three action items you are willing to commit to in your business life and personal life in the next twelve months in the two **twelve-month boxes.**

4. Write three action items you are willing to commit to in your business life and personal life in the next five years in the two **five-year boxes.**

5. Write three action items you are willing to commit to in your business life and personal life in the next ten years in the two **ten-year boxes.**

6. List the ideas that you are not quite ready to commit to, but do not want to throw away, in the **parking lot boxes.** If you are not willing to put the ideas in the parking lot, maybe you should just kill those ideas.

7. Update the list every thirty days and move the action items you accomplish to the **accomplishment boxes.** Let this become a running list (there is great power in reflecting all that you got done, not just all that you have to do).

If there is an idea that you might like to do, but you need to do more research or due diligence, then put that in the parking lot. Independent professionals and solo consultants tend to be idea-generating machines. Celebrate that. There is a place of honor for all those ideas.

The action items can pertain to marketing, selling, and financial aspects of your business. Action item statements begin with verbs. Here are some examples of action items you might include:

- Reshape my profit and loss statement

- Create a client discussion document

- Complete hypersegmentation of database

- Write a book

- Create a menu of services

- Update my website

- Hold a seminar

- Make a speech

- Attend a specific networking event

- Write an article

- Volunteer for a committee with a trade group

- Book registration to attend conference

The personal list can include action items that pertain to having fun, your health, your home, and your spirituality. Here again, action item statements begin with verbs. Here are some examples of personal action items you might include:

- Set a regular date night with spouse

- Attend a baseball game with friends

- Clean the garage

- Take a trip to wine country

- Run a half-marathon

- Attend a religious retreat

- Start a healthy eating program

- Travel to Italy

- See a movie

- Join a gym (and then go to the gym!)

Moving action items from the will-do categories to the accomplishment list creates momentum in your business. It is easy to lose sight of the minor, medium, and major items that get done along the way because our focus is always on what is next and what is still left to do on the list. Give your accomplishments the honor and credit they deserve.

Keep the will-do list where you can find it. Maybe print it out on bright paper and keep it in your planner. Another idea is to place it at eye level on the wall in front of your desk. The important thing is to keep it where you can see it. Then update the list every thirty days. The first day of the month is a great day to do it.

The will-do list directly relates to success. And what is the definition of success? Thank you for asking.

Here is our contrarian view. Success is not determined by results; success is determined by your momentum. Your momentum is determined by how you feel, and how you feel is ultimately determined by the consistent daily application of the best you have within you. In other words, success is giving your personal best. Of course, your personal best can vary from day to day, but that is where our commitment needs to be. The will-do list will bring out your personal best.

PART IV
MARKETING

©Glasbergen
glasbergen.com

"Here are the notes of our last consulting meeting. Some events have been fictionalized for dramatic purposes."

Why should independent consultants worry about marketing? The answer is simple: To make payroll. That means the money to pay the most important person in the world, which is you.

First, let us define terms. By marketing, we mean the process of generating new client leads and then converting those leads into clients. Certain activities get prospects to raise their hands and say they are interested in what you do. Other activities are designed to take that interest and convert it into a signed agreement with a deposit.

Building your consulting practice is the systemized study of attracting, keeping, and growing revenues with clients.

What does the classic research say about how prospective clients decide if they trust independent consultants? Here are the five ways prospects judge you and our views on how marketing applies:[5]

- **Competence.** Knowledge and skill of the professional or consultant and their ability to convey trust and confidence (you demonstrate

---

[5] Aaker, David A. *Strategic Market Management*. New York: John Wiley, 1995.

and prove your expert knowledge by speaking and writing and by the questions you ask prospective clients)

- **Tangibles.** Appearance of physical facilities, communication materials, equipment and personnel (you do this by the appearance of your website, book, and how-to handouts)

- **Empathy.** Caring, individualized attention that a firm provides its clients (educating people to solve problems before they hire you proves you care)

- **Responsiveness.** Willingness to help customers and provide prompt service (when you promise to give people things like special reports and white papers, do it promptly)

- **Reliability.** Ability to perform the promised service dependably and accurately (prospective clients will judge you on how organized your seminars, speeches and website are).

Here are some principles that are important for growing your business.

SIX KINDS OF PROSPECT FIT

Not all prospective clients are created equal. Actually, there are six kinds of client fit. Three are positive and above the line, and three are negative and below the line. The above-the-line fits are:

- **Perfect Fit.** Everything just clicks when you work with these types of people.

- **Great Fit.** Not perfect, but excellent.

- **Good Fit.** Not bad, but not great. You will work with them, but they are not ideal.

And then below the line are:

- **Bad Fit.** Something is just off in the relationship.

- **Wrong Fit.** You are not right for everybody, and you are definitely wrong for these bodies.

- **Horrible Fit.** The client from hell.

Before you try to attract new clients, take a moment to understand who the perfect, great, and good fit clients are for you. Create a profile of your perfect fit client. This involves more than just the demographics of industry, gender, income, location, and age (just to name a few). This means what behaviors, opinions, and attitudes do your perfect fit clients demonstrate. The more you understand what you are looking for, the easier it will be to attract this type of prospect.

On the flip side, understanding what a bad, wrong, and horrible fit client looks like can be extremely helpful. During your interviews the prospects will give clues to identify themselves. Do not work with prospects just because they want to be your clients. To avoid future headaches we suggest being selective by avoiding bad, wrong, and horrible fits as clients.

To attract the new clients you want, you need to prove yourself trustworthy. The best approach we have uncovered is to demonstrate your expertise by giving away valuable information through writing and speaking. That means executing a mix of new contact strategies, which is the focus of the next chapter.

6

EXECUTE A MIX OF NEW CONTACT STRATEGIES

"Most meetings are a waste of time." That is the core message that is building the consulting practice of James Ware, a former Harvard Business School professor.

"We need to bring business meetings into the digital age in the same way that we have reinvented business planning and written communication," says Ware, author of the 2016 book *Making Meetings Matter: How Smart Leaders Orchestrate Powerful Conversations in the Digital Age.*[6]

Independent consultant Ware has invested his entire career in understanding what organizations must do to thrive in a rapidly changing world. His business wisdom comes from deep academic knowledge and

---

[6] Ware, James. *Making Meetings Matter: How Smart Leaders Orchestrate Powerful Conversations in the Digital Age.* Oceanside, CA: Indie Books International, 2016.

more than thirty years of hands-on experience as a senior executive and a change leader who drives corporate innovation.

Ware, who lives in Walnut Creek, California, says leaders should think of a meeting as an improv performance: the most important mindset you can establish is to have a basic plan, but then to be in the moment, reacting both instinctively and creatively to events as they evolve in real time.

A great new-contact strategy for Ware is speaking, but there are no good or bad new-contact strategies. There are seven basic strategies for generating leads. Every independent consultant is different, and all can benefit from a mix of the seven strategies, which are, in alphabetical order:

- **Advertising.** Controlled media channels that you pay to get your message out in collateral, print ads, radio ads, Internet ads, and TV ads.

- **Direct Mail.** Sending e-mail and snail mail to a targeted list of prospects with an offer.

- **Networking.** Attending business events with the intent of meeting others and offering to be of service to them.

- **Publicity.** Obtaining exposure through articles and interviews in newspapers, websites, blogs, books, trade journals, magazines, social media, radio, and television.

- **Showcases.** These include speaking engagements, self-hosted workshops, webinars, teleclasses, online videos, and live webcasts.

- **Telemarketing.** Making phone calls to prospects.

- **Trade Shows.** Purchasing space to set up a booth or table at a sponsored product and service expos.

Ah, but what is the rank order? Many independent professionals and solo consultants do not know there is a body of knowledge about what does and does not work in marketing professional services and consulting. A review of the marketing recommendations of independent consultant marketing experts reveal a recurring theme. Our own twenty years of practical experience in marketing independent consultants support these findings. The best marketing for independent consultants is educational in nature.

Here are the top fourteen new-contact strategies for independent consultants, listed in descending order of effectiveness (these all work, but are rated from worst to best because we like to save the best for last):

THE INADEQUATE SEVEN

14. **Telemarketing by cold calling.** This should be done by a business development person, never a principal (nothing says "trust me" like a cold call). A better approach is what I call warm calling, which is following up showcase event invitations.

13. **Advertising with CD or video brochures.** These can be great lead conversion tools, but they cost too much for lead generation. Instead, stick the videos on your website and on YouTube.

12. **Advertising with printed brochures.** Again, don't spend too much money up front to generate leads. Instead, create these as PDF files that are universally readable and place them on your website.

11. **Advertising by sponsoring cultural/sports events.** Being title sponsor of the right event can have an impact, but it is not the best use of lead-generation dollars.

10. **Advertising in trade magazines.** Isn't it ironic

that none of the great advertising agencies built their clientele by advertising? But if you specialize in an industry and that industry publishes a directory, it is always good to have your firm included. A good idea is to advertise your website or blog that is filled with how-to articles.

9. **Direct mail.** This is the traditional direct mail of a letter and a printed piece, like a response card. Some accountants and financial planners have used this cost-effectively, maybe offering a complimentary consultation (there is a much better form of direct mail—see tactic No. 1).

8. **Publicity that just gets your name out.** While getting your name in the newspaper and trade journals is a cost-effective way to increase awareness about your firm, it doesn't always translate into leads (there is a much better form of publicity—see tactic No. 3).

THE MAGNIFICENT SEVEN

7. **Showcase with workshops based on your proprietary research; support with telemarketing, direct mail, and publicity.** This is the strategy of renting out the ballroom at the local Marriott or Hilton and charging for an all-day

or half-day workshop. Participants should take away a substantial packet of good information from your firm (and a good meal too).

6. **Publicity through the Internet and social media.** This is the water-drip torture school of marketing and the opposite of Spam. By signing up for your e-newsletter lists, prospects are telling you that they are interested in what you have to say, but not ready for a relationship now. These people should receive valuable how-to information and event invitations from you on a monthly basis until they decide to opt-out of the list. For social media, LinkedIn is best.

5. **Networking and trade shows.** This is an excellent way to gather business cards and ask for permission to include them on your e-newsletter list. Focus on building your database.

4. **Networking through community and association involvement.** Everyone likes to do business with people they know, like and trust. You need to get involved and "circulate to percolate," as one Ohio State University professor used to say. Again, focus on building your database.

3. **Publicity through publishing how-to articles**

in books and client-oriented press. Better than any brochure is the how-to article that appears in a publication that your target clients read. Books and blogs are ways to create buzz.

2. **Showcase with how-to speeches at client industry meetings.** People want to hire experts, and an expert by definition is someone who is invited to speak. Actively seek out forums to speak, and list past and future speaking dates on your website. Speak for a fee and speak for free, but target groups comprised almost entirely of your great fit and perfect fit prospects. Shun mixed groups comprised mostly of non-prospects, like Chambers of Commerce.

1. **Showcase with free or low-cost small-scale seminars, support with telemarketing, direct mail, traditional publicity, and social media publicity.** The best proactive tactic you can employ is to regularly invite prospects by mail and e-mail to small seminars or group consultations. If your prospects are spread out geographically, you can do these briefings via the Internet (webinars) or the telephone using a bridge line (teleseminars). These can't be ninety-minute commercials. You need to present valuable in-

formation about how to solve the problems that your prospects are facing, and then a little mention about your services.

USE THE LANGUAGE OF INCREASE

We encourage you to read many of the best-selling works of the classic success authors such as Napoleon Hill, Clement Stone, Dale Carnegie, Og Mandino, Earl Nightingale, Norman Vincent Peale, Zig Ziglar, and today's leading success authors such as Stephen R. Covey, Marshall Goldsmith, Rhonda Byrne and Brian Tracy.

But if you want to go to the source, read a book that inspired all of these authors, titled *The Science of Getting Rich* by Wallace Wattles, written in 1910 and now in the public domain. You can easily find the book for free with a simple Google search. Rhonda Byrne told a *Newsweek* interviewer that her inspiration for creating the 2006 hit film *The Secret* and the subsequent book by the same name, was her exposure to Wattles's *The Science of Getting Rich*. Byrne's daughter, Hayley, had given her mother a copy of the Wattles book to help her recover from a breakdown.

To attract clients, Wattles taught that we need to convey the impression of advancement with everything we do. In addition, we need to communicate that we advance all who deal with us. "No matter how small the transaction, put into it the thought of increase, and make sure the customer is impressed with the thought," wrote Wattles. Create the impression of increase if you want to attract others to you.

According to Wattles, increase is what all people are seeking. His advice was that you should feel that you are getting rich and that in doing so you are making others, like your clients, rich and conferring benefits on all who deal with you. So, when potential clients ask you what you do, please do not give them a list of services and capabilities.

For example, if you are a marketing consultant, use the language of increase to describe your marketing services. You can say that you:

- Improve lead generation

- Help clients maximize revenues

- Increase lead conversion rates

- Improve marketing productivity

- Reduce wasted marketing

- Enable clients to maximize prices

- Help marketing departments exceed goals

Add this language to your conversation, your websites, and your proposals. This is what clients want. There are fortunes to be made by giving clients what they want. Back these statements up with testimonials that document the increase with numbers, percentages, and time factors, and you will be way ahead of the competition.

Here are some real (but not real names) examples:

- "AAA agency has been working strategically with 123 Company partners for over a year now, and they're an integral part of our partner program. We saw great success with partners in the program last year in terms of the retention rate of their new hires. The average retention rate of new employees brought on as part of that program was 70 percent, compared to the typical rate of 20 percent. Overall, the performance of the program more than doubled our first-year expectations. We believe that this is due, in large part, to the work done by your firm, including the use of your

profiling method and your active participation in the recruiting and hiring of the new sales people."
—Maria Gomez, Director of Sales and Marketing, 123 Company

- "In one year, all of the approximately seventy employees we have hired have gone through XYZ personality profile testing and candidate screening. The improved hiring process, combined with improvements in our sales management leadership, has helped our company increase productivity per sales person by a total of 21 percent in the last two years. In addition, while the national average for salesperson turnover in our industry is 40 percent, we've been able to cut that in half with the help of this sales force testing and screening." *—John Smith, President, ABC Company*

- "During the past eighteen months, our work with AAA Agency to train new sales people has helped us double year-over-year revenue growth and employee satisfaction. AAA Agency helps us understand if the candidate is right for us and then how to best manage each employee to make them more productive." *—Kent Clark, President, Big Company*

SKELETON OF KEYWORDS

A skeleton of keywords will help you create client-attracting marketing tools and will improve the quality of the meaningful conversations you have with clients. If you are hiring marketing communications service providers (e.g. advertising copywriters, graphic artists, publicists) to help you, the skeleton of keywords will make their job easier, and that means better results for you.

Know this: Prospects are persuaded more by the depth of your conviction than by any logic you present. Having clarity around these keywords is the best way we know to strengthen that conviction. Here are areas of keywords you need to develop:

- **Company Name.** Don't use your name as the company name. Use a name that clients will know and understand.

- **Outcomes.** What are outcomes you produce for a client?

- **Profit Centers.** What are the various ways you get paid to do the work you do?

- **Needs.** List three client needs you can fill.

- **Wants.** What do clients want that you can provide? List four wants.

- **Results.** What are four results that you provide? These work well as four "more" statements.

Understanding the psychology of prospective clients provides critical evidence of the validity of getting published and giving speeches. Consulting is what economists sometimes call "credence" goods, in that purchasers must place great faith in those who sell the services (the classic research is Bloom, "Effective Marketing for Professional Services," *Harvard Business Review*).[7] You build faith by being an expert who writes articles and gives speeches on how potential clients can solve their problems in general (they hire you for the specifics). With that in mind, let's proceed to the critical step of leveraging your database.

---

[7] Bloom, Paul. "Effective Marketing for Professional Services." *Harvard Business Review*. August 01, 2014. https://hbr.org/1984/09/effective-marketing-for-professional-services.

©Glasbergen
glasbergen.com

GLASBERGEN

"I hope my terminating your consulting contract will in no way affect our marriage."

7

LEVERAGE YOUR DATABASE

Since the 1990s, Nadine Haupt has blazed a successful trail from pit lane to the corporate boardroom—including becoming the first female trackside engineer in IndyCar. Today, as an international professional speaker and leadership consultant, she helps women accelerate their impact, influence, and income to create success and wealth on their terms.

"Finding the right organization and culture to thrive in is a personal endeavor," says Haupt, author of the 2015 book *Fall in Love with Monday Mornings: The Career Woman's Guide to Increasing Impact, Influence and Income.*[8] "What works for some women may not work for others."

As a woman, advises Haupt, you first have to figure out

---

[8] Haupt, Nadine. *Fall in Love with Monday Mornings: The Career Woman's Guide to Increasing Impact, Influence and Income.* Oceanside, CA: Indie Books International, 2015.

what you want. Start with perfecting your inner game. Become clear and focused on your own strengths, values, priorities, and goals. Then, evaluate your organization and culture. You always have choices.

Likewise, to build a practice, an independent consultant needs to figure out what type of clients are wanted. Then the next step is leveraging a database of suspects.

One practice that can help you double your revenues in twelve to twenty-four months is to hypersegment and leverage your database. When it comes to taking advantage of the power of this underutilized business asset, we find independent consultants are at one of four levels. These are, in ascending order:

- **Level 1.** Using an e-mail tool like Constant Contact. Maybe their website gathers e-mail contact information and immediately populates that into an e-mail outreach program like Constant Contact, MailChimp, or Blue Hornet. Prospects, clients, and advocates are all pooled together. Maybe this is complemented by a list of contacts in an MS Outlook contact list.

- **Level 2.** Sending out a mass mailing to the big

list twice a year. Maybe this is a big holiday card mailing or some notice to let them know you exist. Better than just collecting the names and doing nothing with them.

- **Level 3.** Sending an e-newsletter four to twelve times a year. This is at least getting your name out there on a regular basis. Maybe you are sending out tips to everyone and including invitations to speeches or seminars that you are hosting.

- **Level 4.** Practicing hypersegmentation by profit center and by type of prospect or client. Now you are able to tailor messages and offers based on your relationship. You can also target by geographic location and practice the Golden Rule of outreach: only send messages to people that they might like to receive (isn't that how you would like to be treated?).

So how do you get to level 4? Consider the concept of a menu called the Ultimate Results Ladder. Many of the rungs on your ladder would be profit centers. For illustration sake, let's say you have the following:

- Consulting

- Coaching

- Paid seminar

- Free event

- Products like books, audios, and workbooks

Next, think through the various stages of relationship these people might have with you. Here are some basic options.

- Prospects

- Attendees

- Active clients

- Inactive clients

- Buyers

- Volume buyers (Mark sells his book, *Growing Your Business,* by the case)

- Advocates (people who gladly take your phone call and are happy to refer business to you)

This means instead of sticking prospects into one big bucket, you might have twenty-five or more buckets that they belong in. Don't worry that you have not done this in the past. Draw a line in the sand and determine that you will do it from now on.

Here is a possible item for your will-do list, under the category of business/12-month:

Hypersegment my database. This will mean investigating programs like ACT, Goldmine, and Salesforce.com to find the one that is right for you.

©Glasbergen
glasbergen.com

"The phrase 'consulting invoice' is too soft and friendly. We need a new phrase that means pay up or die."

8

NAVIGATE YOUR INTERNET GAME PLAN

"The daunting, ever-increasing speed of change is rapidly altering the relatively simple environment of the late 20th century into a world of exponentially increasing turbulence," say Nick Horney and Tom O'Shea, coauthors of the 2015 book *Focused, Fast & Flexible: Creating Agility Advantage in a VUCA World.*[9] "Being successful in this environment requires a transformation in how an organization operates, in how it thinks about itself, and in how it is led."

In the 1990s, social scientists working with the United States Army War College recognized the ongoing chaos happening around the world and the implications for their mission of preparing our military leaders to understand and lead in this context. They coined

[9] Horney, Nick, and Tom O'Shea. *Focused, Fast & Flexible: Creating Agility Advantage in a VUCA World.* Oceanside, CA: Indie Books International, 2015.

the acronym VUCA as a shorthand way of referring to this environment: Volatile, Uncertain, Complex, and Ambiguous.

North Carolina-based Horney and O'Shea offer a widely-acclaimed best-practices approach built around their trademarked The Agile Model, developed in the course of more than fifteen years of study working with dozens of organizations and thousands of leaders.

In a similar vein, independent consultants need to be agile when it comes to social media if they want to build their practice.

That said, just because you can do many cool things on social media doesn't mean you should. The Internet is the greatest and most efficient time-waster ever invented by humankind.

The following list is what we recommend you focus on to grow your business. The actions are listed in rank order of importance.

- **Google AdWords Keyword Planner.** It is not important how you describe your clients and their interests; the important thing is how they describe themselves. The way to find this for free is through the ultimate free crowdsourcing tool: Google AdWords Keyword Planner. The purpose of this tool is to help Google sell more search engine ad placements. Your purpose for using it is to gauge the popularity of certain descriptions and phrases, based on the number of monthly searches on Google.

- **Website.** Every business needs a website for credibility. How can you trust a business that does not have a website? That said, there are steps you can take to make the site serve you better for lead generation. Number one, keep adding helpful how-to articles to your site on subjects of interest to your prospects. Your website should trade informative materials for e-mail addresses. Use a program like ConstantContact to harvest the e-mails.

- **Blog.** To position yourself as an expert, it is best to blog about your area of expertise. We highly recommend blog/speech/book alignment: the name of the speech or seminar, the name of the book, and the URL should be the same. For instance, Mark is the Growing Your Business expert. He speaks on growing your business, his book is Growing Your Business, and the website URL is www.growingyourbusiness.com. That is alignment.

- **LinkedIn.** Of all the social media sites, LinkedIn is for business, and it is where you need to be. If you have not already joined, then join. To use it as a business development tool, we suggest being liberal with who you link in with. More details in the next section.

- **Facebook.** For many, Facebook is just for friends and family. Others use it to connect with business contacts too. If you choose to go that route, then Facebook is a fine place to announce your new blogs and your upcoming events. As you write and speak more, you become in some ways a mini-celebrity to a small group of people. Many of these are Facebook lurkers who never post, comment, or click the "like" button on your posts. These people just like to keep up on how others are doing, but can also end up referring business your way. For these people, you might reward their interest by posting occasional spots of humor, personal opinions, or tidbits from your travels.

- **Twitter.** In our view, Twitter is for real celebrities, like Lady Gaga and authors like Steve Martin. For professionals and consultants, our recommendation is to get on Twitter and just post tweets about your latest blog.

- **YouTube.** Videos on YouTube are important for two reasons. The first is that YouTube videos are important to the Google search algorithm (not a coincidence, since Google owns YouTube) and videos will raise you up in the search rankings. Secondly, video is rapidly gaining in popularity, especially with the younger generations in the workforce who grew up on video. They would much rather watch a video on a subject than read.

CLOSING THOUGHTS ON LINKEDIN

"Never have so many connected with so much and landed so few new customers," wrote Tom Searcy of Hunt Big Sales, Henry's coauthor of *How to Close a Deal Like Warren Buffett*. Although everybody in the business-to-business world seems to be on the professional networking service, only a rare few have a LinkedIn strategy that gets results. And whose fault is that? Not LinkedIn's. Last time we checked, the potential was staggering. More than 150 million members from over 200 countries. New members are signing up at a rate of two per second. And the demographics are great—the average LinkedIn user is forty-six years old and earns more than $88,000 annually. When it comes to optimizing your use of LinkedIn as a sales tool, there are two different and opposing camps. First, you need to decide which camp you belong in.

> **Camp 1: Link with as many contacts as possible.** This is the "more the merrier" approach. For these people, the larger the network, the better. This approach values quantity over quality, with little regard for whether they know the person they are linking with. These hearty souls might have thousands of contacts in their network.

> **Camp 2: Only link with people who you know, like, and trust.** These are the quality-over-quantity thinkers, who are selective when building their network. When they link with somebody, it means something. These are the "small is beautiful" crowd, with a few hundred or fewer contacts.

There is no right or wrong way to use LinkedIn. As an author and someone who does a lot of public speaking, Tom is in the first camp, with some 7,000 LinkedIn contacts. His goal is to make himself accessible. By contrast, he has a client who jealously guards his LinkedIn network.

"You have to pass muster to join his elite

team," says Searcy. "He wants everyone in his network to know that they have his personal endorsement."

Henry and Mark are in Camp 1. But we live in a world of more than one right answer.

Whichever camp you choose, there are several ways to make sure you are not the weakest link in your LinkedIn chain of contacts:

1. **Fill out your profile.** Don't try to get away with a bare-bones profile. Make sure to fully fill out your profile. Being the kind of person who does things half way is not a good signal to send out to sales prospects. Do enter as much information as possible. Do put in keywords that relate to what you sell under "Specialties." Do add your photo, because it makes referral sources and prospects feel more connected to you.

2. **Update your status line.** This is your chance to broadcast serious business news—about you. But don't treat LinkedIn like Facebook or Twitter; please do not post trivial status updates.

3. **Get recommendations.** No profile is complete without some good recommenda-

tions. One savvy LinkedIn user once told me, "How can I trust someone if they can't get three people to say good things about them on LinkedIn?"

4. **Prove you know them.** When you are inviting someone to link with you, take the time to explain how you are connected.

5. **Research prospects.** We assume you have a target filter for the kinds of companies you want to sell to. From that filter, we assume you have some companies you are actively researching. LinkedIn is perfect for this. The best thing about the company information on LinkedIn is that it comes straight from members, not from corporate spokespeople.

Overall, understand that LinkedIn is a community where karma counts. Your mantra should be, "I give before I get." Answer questions for others. Respond to requests that you receive. Give recommendations to those you have done good business with. Relationships lead to sales, and you can enhance relationships quickly and easily when you interact in a digital business marketplace like LinkedIn.

9

LISTEN CAREFULLY, RESPOND APPROPRIATELY

Chris Stiehl, an independent research consultant who calls himself "The Listening Coach," has built a career on helping people listen.

"Your prospects are talking, but are you really listening?" asks Stiehl, a human-factors-engineer who has worked for the Cadillac division of General Motors, the United States Coast Guard, and even the Nuclear Regulatory Commission to analyze the Three Mile Island accident and make recommendations back in 1979.

"At Cadillac, we spent about $20,000 on a Voice-of-the-Customer project that saved the company $3 million per year going forward," says Stiehl, who notes that a lack of listening is not just a North American problem. "We have conducted listening research in India, China,

Brazil, Singapore, Kuala Lumpur and Switzerland, as well as Canada and the United States."

During conversations with a prospect, the goal of an independent consultant should be to monopolize the listening. A good rule of thumb is to listen 80 percent of the time and talk 20 percent.

These are the three proven steps for success when it comes to listening carefully and responding appropriately to prospects:

1. **Identify the issue.** What is on their mind? Why did they reach out to you? What are their goals, what assets do they have in place, and what are their roadblocks? Ask questions to find out and listen carefully.

2. **Listen for the prospect's mindset.** This is not about good and bad people; actually, this is about how they view the world at this point in time. Are they a thinker, a doer, a struggler, or an achiever? Again, ask questions and listen carefully.

3. **Respond in a way that meets what that person wants and needs.** To respond appropriately requires matching your language to the mindset of

the prospect. Say the appropriate words that the thinker, doer, struggler, or achiever needs to hear.

LISTENING RESPONDING TO THE FOUR MINDSETS

You will find that prospects fall into one of four mindsets when it comes to buying your products and engaging your services. If you can identify the mindset of your prospect, and then respond in a manner that meets what that prospect wants and needs at that moment, you will go a long way toward building trust and rapport with your prospects. This is the ultimate communication tool, and it is easy. It simply requires that you listen carefully.

THINKERS

A Thinker is someone who is thinking about buying your products and services. If you can understand this and respond accordingly, you can be of much better service.

Examples of what Thinkers say:

- I am thinking about buying a car.

- We've been thinking about remodeling our . . .

- I think I will join a health club.

- Maybe we should work with a financial planner.

- I was wondering about . . .

When you hear statements like these, then your Thinker flag should go up. If you know what these people want and need at this moment, you have it made. Thinkers want to make a decision and need information in order to make an informed decision. Do not try to sell to these prospects. Ask them how long they have been thinking about this. What kind of information are they looking for that would help them to make this decision? What is the timeframe for making the decision? If you move quickly to sell these prospects, you run the risk of overwhelming and thus alienating them.

DOERS

A Doer is someone who has made the decision to buy your products and services—hopefully from you. If you understand this and respond accordingly, you will have a better chance of making the sale today.

Examples of what Doers say:

- I've made the decision to buy a new car.

- We're going to switch accounting firms.

- I am going to lose ten pounds in ninety days.

- Let's find someone to manage our money.

- I am going to start my business this summer.

When you hear statements like these, then your Doer flag should go up. If you know what these people want and need at this moment, you have it made. They want action, and they need to hear your sense of urgency. Move quickly with these prospects. Ask them how soon they would like to take possession or get the ball rolling, or what the target date is. Take charge of these sales. Keep an eye on being productive and don't waste time and you will delight your prospects, and you will stand head and shoulders above your competition.

STRUGGLERS

A Struggler is someone who is in a momentary period of struggle. Everyone falls into this mindset from time to time, depending on what issue or challenge is before us. If you can understand this prospect and respond accordingly, you can manage the sale properly or even let this one go. You don't have to sell everyone.

Examples of what Strugglers say:

- You charge how much?

- I'd never pay that price!

- What kind of a deal can I get?

- What is your hourly rate?

- I am *sooo* busy.

- I just don't have time.

When you hear statements like these, then your Struggler flag should go up. If you know what these people want and need at this moment, you have it made. They want a quick fix, and they need a new perspective. Be careful not to get wrapped up in their problems, or you might find yourself in a moment of struggle. Draw this person out and help them think things through before they make a decision. You may need to provide a wake-up call or a new perspective. Don't make any mistakes and stick to your terms. If you bend the rules and go too far in order to accommodate this prospect, it will come back to haunt you.

ACHIEVERS

An Achiever is someone who focuses on outcomes. Achievers are focused on what will happen when they put your products to good use or experience the results and benefits of your services. With most Achievers, what you charge is likely to be perceived as an investment in the outcomes provided rather than a cost for your products or services.

Examples of what Achievers say:

- We're looking for someone we can work with.

- I'd like to work with someone who will . . .

- I'd rather pay a little more and make sure . . .

- It's important we find someone we can trust.

- Our suppliers are an important part of our team.

When you hear statements like this, then your Achiever flag should go up. Make sure you respond accordingly. These prospects want teamwork and need a resource. Here is your opportunity to build relationships that can last. Find out what is most important to them and how your competitors worked with them. See if you can uncover the pros and cons of your competitors. Achievers will give you prescriptions for succeeding or failing. Stay close, and never take them for granted. If you do, you will lose, and they will look for another resource they can put on their team. Don't allow that day to ever happen.

PAIN-INTO-GAIN RIDDLE

Your target prospects experience their own unique frustrations and pains. As the old adage states, "People don't care what you know until they know that you care." Truly identifying your prospect's predicament tells them that you understand and empathize with them.

THE PAIN-INTO-GAIN LISTENING RIDDLE

How will prospects hire you unless they trust you?

How, in turn, will they trust ideas they have not heard?

How, in turn, will they hear without someone to speak?

How, in turn, will you speak unless you have a solution?

How, in turn, will you have a solution unless you understand their pain?

How will you understand their pain unless you listen carefully?

How will you prove you listened unless you respond appropriately?

The listening coach Stiehl says that when you have conversations with prospects, there are ten questions you might work into the conversation:

1. Can you describe for me the ideal experience with a _____ (your line of consulting). How do most compare to this ideal?

2. Can you describe for me a recent time that the experience was less than ideal?

3. What are the three most important aspects of doing business with a _____?

4. If I said a _____ was a good value, what would that mean to you?

5. Other than money, what does dealing with a _____ cost you (time, hassle, effort, etc.)?

6. What is the biggest pain about working with a _____?

7. Would you recommend a _____ to a friend or colleague? Why, or why not?

8. How does working with a _____ help you make money?

9. What does a _____ do really well?

10. If you had the opportunity to work with a _____ again, would you? Why, or why not?

So, what can an independent consultant do to maximize the number of conversations they have with prospects? That is the subject of the final part of this book.

PART V

MYSTERY SOLVED: THE NUMBER ONE MARKETING TOOL AND STRATEGY

©Glasbergen
glasbergen.com

"I should have been a consultant. I spent years climbing the corporate ladder, only to find out it was scaffolding for the new corporate headquarters."

Being a published author is the quickest path to becoming an expert who attracts new clients. Publishing a book and speaking are the core of the Educating Expert Model employed by many successful independent consultants. So why doesn't every independent consultant have a book?

Thanks to new technologies, today it is not only possible to produce a professional-looking copy of your book for $5,000 to $10,000, but you can also market the book (traditional version and e-book) through reputable sales channels.

A decade ago, there weren't many options for independent consultants to get into print as a book author. If a traditional publisher wasn't interested in your manuscript, your only other option was to spend tens of thousands of dollars with a subsidy press or custom printer. (To us, that is the S-word: self-published.) And then, without ready distribution, good luck trying to *sell* the books.

But that has all changed, because alternative publishers are able to print both paperback and hardcover books as they're needed due to the bold new digital publishing technology known as "print-on-demand." Going digital allows books to be produced in small quantities—even one at a time—almost instantaneously. No longer does publishing require behemoth offset presses, hangar-size warehouses, and fleets of trucks.

These alternative, niche publishers have made a conscious decision to offer their services to everyone, rather than cede control to an elite clique of editors and agents, as is generally the case in traditional publishing. While incoming manuscripts are checked for formatting before a new title goes online, alternative publishers do not edit for style and content. These consultants do not make value judgments about the literary merit of books. The author decides what the public reads, and the public decides if it makes good reading or not. It is a purely market-driven approach and allows almost anyone to make a new book available to millions of readers at a small fraction of the cost of traditional publishing methods.

There are challenges with this approach, of course. Because print-on-demand books are not typically stocked on bookstore shelves, authors need to do a good job of marketing through publicity, direct mail, and the Internet. But if you are a nonfiction author willing to be a self-promoter whose book targets an identifiable market, then alternative publishing may be right for you.

Print-on-demand has enormous implications for professionals, consultants, writers, readers, publishers, and retailers. Because books are produced on demand, there are never wasted copies ("remaindered," as they used to be dubbed in the old days). Paperbacks and hardcover books are priced competitively, with authors receiving royalties of 30 percent or more. For Kindle books, the royalty is 70 percent. Compare those with traditional publishing industry royalty standards of 5 to 15 percent, and the appeal becomes a bit clearer still.

What about the writing? If you can write articles, then you can write a book. And if you can't, you can always hire a freelance ghostwriter to help you do it. (Ghosts are not so scary; the thoughts are yours, but the ghost will do the heavy lifting of organizing and writing.)

SHOWCASING WITH SEMINARS

You may have a great idea for a small-scale seminar to attract potential clients. But it's quite another thing to pull it off successfully. The myriad of small details involved can make or break an event. Here are some recommendations to maximize the success of your next lead-generation seminar.

- Develop a checklist and timeline for pre/post seminar activities.

- Decide if this will be a free briefing or an event that you will charge for (there is a time and a place for both).

- Use informal research to pretest topics to make sure the one you choose has the most appeal to your target audience.

- Make sure the letters or invitations you use reflect a first-class image for your firm.

- Confirm registrations forty-eight hours before the event by e-mail.

- Deliver seminar content that is of real value to clients, not a thinly disguised sales pitch for your services.

- After the seminar, make it easy for the potential client to contact you in the future by sending a thank you e-mail/letter with phone number and Web address.

- Conduct an organized follow up five to ten days after the seminar or event in an effort to start a dialogue with potential clients.

- Measure how much the seminars cost and how much revenue was ultimately generated to calculate your return on investment (ROI).

FINDING PLACES TO SPEAK

Would you like to add $100,000 or more to your annual income? Then showcase your expertise with paid speeches.

One day, Henry was taking his two teenage sons to Disneyland. The night before, a program chairman had called Henry to ask a favor because his breakfast speaker had cancelled. So, along the way to Disneyland, Henry stopped to give a speech to a group of Orange County business owners while his boys munched on a fast-food breakfast in the car.

That speech eventually generated five-figures' worth of revenue for Henry. He picked up various paid speeches and consulting work as a result of that talk. But the speaking fee was only a few hundred dollars. As Henry came back to the car, he tucked the honorarium check (more *honor* than *rarium*) in the center console. His older son asked about the check and Henry told him that these business owners actually paid him to market his services to them.

"Sweet," said his son. "That is the perfect crime."

FIVE CONSULTANT STRATEGIES TO GET PAID TO MARKET

Here are some more examples of this perfect crime, committed by independent consultant clients we are especially proud of.

One consultant we coach complained that he wasn't getting any consulting business for the past six months from a Fortune 500 client. There are more ways to get paid than straight consulting, we told him.

Often, companies that don't have money for consultants have money in their training budgets. So, he organized a seminar, and held the event near the company's headquarters and sold eleven seats for $600 each to that same Fortune 500 client. After the event, several attendees found some budget, and he landed about $75,000 in consulting projects. Later, he charged another client $1,500 (he is worth much more) for a ninety-minute talk at a company meeting that netted him consulting contracts in the five figures.

Another independent consultant we coach was able to double her revenue in a year (we're talking over $100,000 more) just by having different conversations about her pricing with potential clients. Actually, when she raised her rates, it was a signal to her right-fit audience that she was in demand and a hot commodity. But alas, she wanted to make even more money. She soon realized there are only so many hours in a week (168, to be precise) and only so much you can charge clients per hour. To increase her revenue, she needed to leverage her time. She created some independently published guide books and started offering her expertise through workshops. That leveraged her time and created new streams of revenue.

Here are five potential perfect crimes: being paid to market your services. These are venues that write checks to consultants to speak:

- **Keynotes and breakouts at association and trade group meetings.** A keynote is typically thirty to ninety minutes and usually focuses on a broad topic of interest to all attendees. A breakout session is one of the side sessions at a meeting and lasts from forty-five to ninety minutes. This is the glamour field of professional speaking. Competition is fierce, and the big fees go to celebrities (the group is trading on the speaker's star status to attract attendees). We put speaking at Vistage groups (formerly TEC) of about a dozen company presidents for half a day at $500 per speech in this category.

- **Corporate training**. These are typically half-day or full-day seminars and workshops conducted for a private client, usually a corporation, for a group of its employees. This might be the most lucrative field for speaking, because there are many companies that have training budgets. Several clients who make hundreds speaking for Vistage make thousands when they deliver the same presentations to companies. This one-two punch has made several clients an extra $100,000 per year.

- **Sponsoring your own public seminars**. This is typically a full-day seminar or workshop where registration is open to the public. You market the event and earn a profit (or loss). This business is about putting fannies in seats. Many times it is a break-even proposition getting the attendees there, and then you make your real money selling information products and consulting services at the back of the room after the event is over. Fees can range from $800 to $1,000 per day, per attendee, all the way down to my three-hour Lunch-and-Learn seminars, which are priced at $25.

- **Teaching at colleges and for public seminar companies.** An alternative to running the seminar yourself is to find a sponsor. This might be for a company like Career Tracks or The Learning Annex. Or you might approach the adult education marketplace through a college or university extended studies program. Typically, you might earn 25 percent of what the students pay, all the way up to $1,000 for a day.

- **Speaking at fundraising workshops where you split the gate.** Another alternative to running the seminar yourself is to approach a trade group or association and offer to stage a fundraising seminar. They promote the event to their constituents, and you agree to split the profits (typically 50/50 and you may or may not offer them 10 percent of any informational products like books and CDs that you sell in the back of the room after the event).

AND IN CLOSING

Truly, the best proactive consultant marketing strategy is to regularly showcase your expertise by giving informative and entertaining talks in front of targeted groups of potential right-fit clients. Speak for free and speak for a fee, if it is your pure, right-fit audience.

The trick is knowing whom to contact to get booked as a speaker and developing a topic that will draw the right audience. Nobody said it is going to be easy to be a published author and a popular speaker. But it sure beats hoping, wishing, and praying the phone will ring. We wish you success.

APPENDIX A

AXIOMS AND ADAGES

- A book is the number one marketing tool, and speaking is the number one marketing strategy.

- Being happily published means you must be happy with your book. No one else really matters.

- Better to write than get it right.

- Change your language and it will change your game.

- Consistency trumps commitment. What you do daily is more important than what you do once in a while.

- Cultivate advocates, your true champions and cheerleaders.

- Don't make yourself the hero of your stories. The client is the hero; he or she overcomes a nemesis challenge, and you are the mentor character who gave them the advice they needed to succeed.

- Don't just write a book. Write the *right* book.

- Every first of the month, you get to celebrate a happy new year.

- Fear is your friend. Fear is your enemy. Fear is your frenemy.

- Having yearly goals is just stupid. The secret of success is the phrase "every thirty days."

- Humans are hardwired to respond to eight great stories: monster, underdog, comedy, tragedy, quest, mystery, rebirth, and escape. (See Henry's book *Persuade With a Story!*)

- If a marketing strategy doesn't work, it is not the strategy's fault.

- In a strategy call or coffee chat, offer the prospect the chance to get clarity on four subjects: their goals, their assets, their roadblocks, and how others have gotten from where they are to where they want to go.

- In California, we say "the universe rewards activity;" in the Midwest, we say "God helps those who help themselves."

- In marketing, the magic is in the mix.

- Know your target, then seek out target-rich environments.

- Like hangs out with like.

- Marketing is an art, and selling is a skill.

- Never say you are "following up." Instead, say you are circling back to answer any questions.

- No more getting ready to get ready.

- No one connection will make you, and no one connection will break you.

- Only tell stories if you want to persuade people. If you just want them to think it over, give them lots of facts and figures.

- Perfect is the enemy of done.

- Plant three seeds a day; plant three seeds per prospect.

- Publishing a book is the starting line, not the finish line.

- Repeat after me: "I am happy and grateful money comes to me in increasing amounts on a consistent monthly basis."

- Reset your counters to zero every day, every week, and every month.

- Start your outreach with, "If you would be open to a conversation..."

- Success is determined by momentum; momentum is determined by how you feel; how you feel is determined by the consistent daily application of your personal best.

- The *how* always follows the *want*.

- The magic word is "if." *If* is an honoring word, not a sales word. Saying "if" is like a soft knock on the door.

- The most important number is what you want to earn every thirty days.

- The reason behind marketing is to make payroll: yours.

- The secret of writing is applying seat of the pants to the seat of the chair.

- The trifecta is a book title, speech title, and domain of the same name.

- Trade proposals for an agreement to have a meaningful conversation.

- Trade your days for your dreams, not for your survival.

- Use the nine best practices to create a booking machine.

- We find money for what we want; so do clients, corporations, and associations.

- When setting monthly goals, look for numbers divisible by four, twelve, and thirty.

- When someone offers you something great, pause three seconds for dignity and say: "Thank you for asking."

- When you invent something great, name it after yourself, like the LeBlanc Success by Nine Matrix.

- Your wrong fit prospects are not only wrong; they make you wrong.

©Glasbergen
glasbergen.com

"I am not a guru, but I am a consultant."

APPENDIX B

ABOUT THE AUTHOR

HENRY DEVRIES

Henry DeVries is the CEO (chief encouragement officer) of Indie Books International, a company he cofounded in 2014. He works with independent consultants who want to attract more high-paying clients by marketing with a book and speech.

As a speaker, he trains business development teams and business leaders on how to sell more services by persuading with a story.

He is also the president of the New Client Marketing Institute, a training company he founded in 1999. He is the former president of an Ad Age 500 advertising and PR agency and has served as a marketing faculty member and assistant dean of continuing education at the University of California, San Diego.

In the last ten years, he has helped ghostwrite,

edit, and coauthor more than 300 business books, including his McGraw-Hill bestseller, *How to Close a Deal Like Warren Buffett*—now in five languages, including Chinese. He has a monthly column with Forbes.com. He earned his bachelor's degree from UC San Diego, his MBA from San Diego State University, and has completed certificate programs at the Harvard Business School.

As a result of his work, consultants and business owners get the four *B*s: more bookings, more blogs, more buzz, and a path and plan to more business.

On a personal note, he is a baseball nut. A former Associated Press sportswriter, he has visited forty major league ball parks and has four to go before he "touches 'em all."

His hobby is writing comedy screenplays that he hopes will one day be made into films.

To contact Henry DeVries to purchase multiple copies of this book or to book him as a speaker (or invite him to a baseball game), you may e-mail him at henry@ indiebooksintl.com, or call him at 619-540-3031.

OTHER BOOKS BY HENRY DEVRIES

Self-Marketing Secrets (with Diane Gage)

Pain-Killer Marketing (with Chris Stiehl)

Client Seduction (with Denise Montgomery)

Closing America's Job Gap (with Mary Walshok and Tappan Monroe)

Marketing the Marketers

How to Close a Deal Like Warren Buffett (with Tom Searcy)

Marketing with a Book

Persuade with a Story!

APPENDIX C

ABOUT THE AUTHOR

MARK LEBLANC

Mark LeBlanc, the founder of Growing Your Business and cofounder and chairman of Indie Books International, has special expertise on the core issues that independent consultants face on a daily basis and is qualified to address audiences of five to fifty to 500, and more. He can deliver an inspirational can-do keynote, a content-rich general session, hands-on workshop, and/or a multi-day program.

His flagship presentation and book, *Growing Your Business!*, are ideal for addressing how to sell more products and services. Attendees walk away feeling more focused, able to attract more prospects, stimulate more referrals, and ultimately, craft a plan for generating more business.

LeBlanc has been on his own virtually his entire adult life, owned several businesses, and now speaks and writes on the street-smart strategies for achieving in times of challenge and change. His is a comprehensive, one-of-a kind, business development philosophy that has the right blend of wisdom, strategies, insights, and ideas that can be implemented immediately.

LeBlanc's book *Never Be the Same* was inspired by walking the 500-mile Camino de Santiago pilgrimage across Northern Spain. Audiences have been captivated by the self-management and self-leadership lessons learned along the trek. In 2017, LeBlanc walked the 500-mile Camino de Santiago for the third time.

LeBlanc is a seasoned veteran with the National Speakers Association and served as the national President in 2007-2008. His strategies and ideas are distributed to Chambers of Commerce executives and Chamber members around North America. In addition, he is the Founder of The Y.E.S. (Young Entrepreneurs Succeed) Foundation. Its sole purpose is to give $3,000 grants to entrepreneurs under thirty.

To contact Mark LeBlanc to purchase multiple copies of his books or to book him as a speaker, you may e-mail him at mark@growingyourbusiness.com, or call him at 612-339-4890.

78081610R00082

Made in the USA
Columbia, SC
09 October 2017